FACING TOWN AND GOWN: FUTURIZING CONNECTION AND COMMUNITY

PRINCESS ANNE, MARYLAND

DR. AMY HAGENRATER-GOODING

THE FACING PROJECT PRESS

THE FACING PROJECT PRESS

An imprint of The Facing Project

Muncie, Indiana 47305

facingproject.com

First published in the United States of America by The Facing Project Press, an imprint of The Facing Project and division of The Facing Project Gives Inc., 2024.

First paperback edition April 2024

Cover design by Shantanu Suman

Photos by Deb Laforest

Library of Congress Control Number: 2024935364

ISBN: 979-8-9860961-9-3 (paperback)

ISBN: 979-8-9902900-0-6 (eBook)

Printed in the United States of America

10 9 8 7 6 5 4 3 2 1

CONTENTS

INTRODUCTION

Pulling off of route 13 and into the sleepy town of Princess Anne, you'd be unsure you were entering the home of the University of Maryland Eastern Shore. From the south, you might take the shortcut past the high school, drive down Main Street where the only activity seems to be at the small post office to the left or the fire hall at the town's second traffic light. From the north, you would see a welcome sign, both to Princess Anne and UMES, but the campus sits far back from the main highway and the new crosswalk leading to the booming new Royal Farms across the highway might be the only indicator that there is a reason to take the trek to the left and weave around the traffic circle, arriving at an institution where over 2500 students work and live, creating their own community nestled in this small, unassuming town far from their home, for many of them. This community in this Eastern Shore enclave extends beyond the university and Somerset County to the surrounding rural counties of Worcester and Wicomico. For students, it's their community for the four years they are here; for the professionals who work and live in the area, it is home.

Coming here can be like stepping back in time. The driving is slower, the pace is relaxed, and the attitudes and beliefs in some pockets can seem almost retrograde. Moving here in 2008 had me marked as a "come here," a designation I never heard of until I learned that this place can thrive on division, categorization. A "from here" achieves a certain rootedness to the shore and a kind of mindset that legacy can only achieve. It can be alienating, this divide, but not as much as another, the racial lines that are still somewhat drawn in the area. I will never forget unloading our U-Haul in our move from Pennsylvania and folks stopping by saying hi. My interior monologue thought "this really is the friendliest town on the shore," but I later learned this was also a sizing up, a measuring of my place in this space. One older grandfatherly type pulled up in his truck and welcomed us heartily. Standing in the driveway, I was convinced I had misheard him, that voice so confident he could speak freely to strangers about how happy he was our family was moving in and not another. I wish I could say he knew us and that he said his welcome without the pejorative slur after his assertion. He didn't know us, and he didn't hold his tongue.

I am often reminded of Chimamanda Ngozi Adiche's "Danger of a Single Story" whereby she talks about the problem of stereotyping based on one singular narrative of a place or a people. There is danger in a solitary narrative, but power there, too, and that's how we came to The Facing Project.

Students in Advanced Composition partnered with community leaders and professionals to learn about their experiences coming to the shore, learning in the UMES community, or valuing the role of education as a way to make a change. Words matter and having the opportunity to step into someone else's story in the telling of their story is a powerful way to establish a new community of learning and growing. Our stories help us bridge our way to a future where we can know more intimately. That is true here where you will meet UMES college students (at one time) who returned to the university bridging their past to give back in the present. There are leaders in the community who took the hidden curriculum they were prescribed and laid it bare. These stories are a testimony to the way narrative, the way "I" can build a bridge to a better future, especially when we look through the "I"s of another.

Dr. Amy Hagenrater-Gooding

How We Grow

James Jones's Story as Told to Adin Clarke

I grew up in a time of segregation to integration. I was brought up in a Methodist church with an amazing black preacher named Charles Tindley. But when I turned six years old, our church got shut down. This was when our family moved to a Baptist church with Dr. Isaac Jenkins. Growing up, I went to an all-black school called Steven Long Elementary up until the sixth grade. This is when integration started to take place. From seventh to ninth grade, I went to Worcester High School. In this short span of time, I went from seeing all the people who looked like me to people who looked as if they hated me.

I was not always the man I am today. When I moved to that school, I was constantly fighting the other kids. I had to. I was not going to take the disrespect and racism that they would thrust upon me. I continued to fight for myself up until the eleventh grade when the guidance counselor called my friends and I into her office. What this guidance counselor said may have altered my entire way of thinking. She said that if we never returned to school, she would give us all a certification of attendance for all twelve years. What kind of shit is that? Not a diploma, but a certificate that says I went there all twelve years. It was then that I changed my point of view. I went from starting fights to breaking them up. This is also about the time I started to serve God--for me. Not for my parents or because it was what was expected of me,

1

but because I wanted to. I graduated in 1971. The last all-black class was in 1970–I was one year off.

After I graduated, I briefly went to college in Silver Spring, but would then go to the Air Force. Back then, the draft was alive and well and this was during the Vietnam War, so instead of possibly being drafted, handed a gun, and expected to start shooting at people, I chose to go into the Air Force. I spent thirteen years in the Air Force and twenty years away from Pocomoke. That time away in California, things were different. People were more open and accepting, even friendly. The Air Force was educational and life-changing. It showed me how to be the man I am today.

I have been in ministry for twenty-four years now. I am also a tailor, an activist, and I help with groups like CAUCUS and NABVET (National Association for Black Veterans). I am busy, to say the least. NABVET helps black veterans. Our goal is to enhance the lifestyles of all veterans through service. I am proud of CAUCUS which is all about giving back to the community, spreading awareness of the active racism that is still going on in our community, and the injustice still going on in our schools. I feel as if we are making a real change in our community. We have helped fight many injustices within the black community and I am proud to say that thirty of our thirty-two cases have been won.

I am adamant about helping the youth. Going through the unfair treatment I had as a child, I would never want anyone to go through the unfair prejudice and judgment I went through based on the color of their skin. When I started at that new school, those teachers were awful. They didn't even view me as worthy to teach. They thought they were blessing me by just letting me hear them teach. They would often tell me if you get it, good, if not, oh well. This treatment filled me with anger and grief, thus the fights. To help kids who might be going through the same issues I was, I started a group called Seven to Fourteen. This is a group of kids at the church and the goal is to get kids to find encouragement in religion and a better way of life.

I grew up in a time of segregation to integration. This transition helped me in many ways. Sometimes someone needs to be broken down in order to build themselves up to become a better person. I think that everything that happened in my life had a purpose, and I am glad that it has made me into the man I am today. A man who values God and helps give back to his community.

MR. KNOW-IT-ALL

EARL HOLLAND'S STORY AS TOLD TO ANGEL MANSFIELD

S ome people would call it knowing it all, but really, I just like facts. Growing up, there was no internet just yet, but I was never really an outside kid. No more than the arcade at the mall here and there. I was more into the game shows. My parents divorced when I was 10. Co-parenting wasn't that bad though. There were always two Christmases, two birthdays, etc., so I don't see it as too bad. I have never been outdoorsy, so game shows, learning and reading history, and just watching TV were my thing. I was all for the facts. No real sports until I was 12. Growing up in the '80s in Salisbury, Maryland, there wasn't as much to do then as there is to do today. I was born in Salisbury, spent 25% of my life in Snow Hill, Maryland, and then seven years in Delaware. One thing that never changed was interacting and sharing my love for writing and storytelling with others. With my past experience as a journalist and newspaper reporter, I've always felt that people have a story to tell.

When I think of Princess Anne, I think of my whole college experience. Growing up in Salisbury, I never really went to Princess Anne until I went to college, despite the towns only being 20 minutes apart. I attended UMES with the mindset of getting my bachelor's in English with a minor in communication, and that's just what I did. I remember my first day like it was yesterday. Things were different than they are today. Back then, the liquor and convenience store known today as Junior's used to be a Shore Stop. Half the buildings on campus weren't even there yet. I started UMES in August of 2001, but when I was 21 years old, my junior year, I can remember Hazel still being built, Kiah was the math building, and almost every English class was in Wilson. All the old buildings we know now were all considered new then.

Throughout this whole process, I was guided by my professor, Marilyn Buerkle. Even though she doesn't work here anymore, and is retired, she worked at the university with the broadcasting students. Even in college, I was still all about the facts. From 2001 to 2005, I was part of the Honda Campus All-Star Challenge quiz bowl team. The Honda team is a campus-based organization for students who like trivia, who are know-it-alls, who can reel off quick facts, and use their knowledge to compete against other HBCUs.

But my true calling has always been creeping in my ear like a ghost. I will always say that my career calling is public relations. I started working for the *Daily Times* newspaper in Salisbury as a reporter first out of college, making little to nothing. I loved the job and the opportunities it brought me, but it wasn't really reliable. Left and right, people were getting laid off right in front of me. I needed a change; I couldn't be next. I wanted more for myself, so I sought out the opportunity. I also did radio on and off for 15 years. Then I got this urge. I needed to give back to my university. And I did in July 2022.

I started back at UMES as an employee and I loved it. There have been many ups and downs, just like any other job, although my biggest accomplishment is seeing the pitches my team and I made for the school get picked up and spread out. People from all over can see my pitch. Things are going well for me now. I am happily married, going on 11 years now, with a daughter who is two and a newborn son. I am also in the second year as the coach for the quiz bowl team at UMES. As a journalist, I have won six awards, including four MDDC (Maryland, Delaware, DC Press Association) awards, not to mention being an eight-time winner on the game show, Sports Jeopardy. Now I'm sharing facts with my team and other students. What do you want to know?

BRANCHING OUT

AMBER GREEN'S STORY AS TOLD TO DAYAUNI JEFFRIES

I would say that I did not pick the shore, and that the shore picked me. Seeing how different everything was down here from where I came from, D.C and near Brandywine, was really a revelation. I hated being down here. Everything would weigh on me. Why is stuff like this still happening down here? That's not how the world works, I would think to myself. You know that Beyoncé song "I Was Here"? That was my motivation. One of the opening lines is "Leave something to remember, so they won't forget." I wanted to leave something for the community saying I was here. And to make an impact, you must become a leader.

I noticed much of the time that the youth who are marginalized, who come from low-income communities, are Black and Hispanic youth that do not have the opportunities to have a leadership program. They do not have anyone to look up to or something to look forward to and keep them going. They tend to be more inclined to hear their form of activism through a song or poem, but never firsthand.

Have you ever heard of the Harlem Renaissance? No? Well, I am a huge fan myself. Zora Neale Hurston: I love her. Langston Hughes? I call him my fairy Godfather. Seeing how they made a change in this world using their poems and creating these literary works of art, that is exactly what we needed to do to make a change through art. Fenix came out of that need or want. I would say to leave something here and that for the world to be the best version of itself, we need to start empowering our youth to use their creative talents to do the same thing as these creative artists and speak with their passion. I wanted to give the youth out here something that will help them have a "stepping stone" in leaving their mark—much like I did.

That is Fenix, and from 2013 till now, ten years later we are a leader in the tri-state area, not just the little old county of Wicomico. I am talking about the whole lower eastern shore. Not to mention we are the only org on the shore that services homeless youth, and that is because we saw the amount of youth who were out on the streets and decided we needed to do something about it. That makes me mad now that I think about it. So many homeless youth for so long and it took me, a 23-year-old college student from way across the bridge to do something about it. Now do not get me wrong; the ten years weren't easy. Within those 10 years I faced problems just like any other black woman faces when trying to do something for their community. I faced issues like racism, misogyny, ageism, dealing with my own mental journey, having my son, falling in love, and falling out of love. Just really the ins and outs of life. In those 10 years I have been able to appreciate these challenges.

Covid was one of the best times for my organization. Being locked down for two years and seeing the same faces all day every day made me hungry for more from myself. Being locked down in a place that was not comfortable made me hungry to get out. The youth center opened during Covid. The pandemic really shifted me and Fenix into a new direction. Personally, I needed to be tired of the place I was in and needed to get out.

People weren't hiring and what were people doing if they could not find jobs? They were making their own businesses, so I went ahead and took my non-profit and started treating it like a business. I started networking and talking to the right people, so much so to the point that in the middle of Covid we got a 100,000 dollar grant to open a second youth center.

That was the first time I was able to pay myself as a founder and executive director. Mind you, by this point we have been an organization since 2013. That is when I realized that, hey, this is a real business. Everything skyrocketed. It was crazy. We grew from a small organization raising 10,000 dollars a year to an organization who was getting 100,000 dollars a year in government contracts to provide services to homeless youth. It was amazing seeing all my hard work really pay off and make a difference in people's lives.

All the youth I have encountered over the years are now in their twenties. I met them when they were 15 or 16. And when you have known someone from their teenage years and watched them grow and change and see them benefit from all the seeds you have planted with them, and see that change you so longed for in the community unfold for yourself, it is such an amazing feeling.

I recently ran into one of the young girls I had been helping when she was in high school. She was part of the LGBT community. It was Pride Day I believe, and she had worn her flags and everything to school that day. That day, she and the other students participating in the event were hit so hard with bullying, and I am talking about not just from the students, but the teachers as well. It was horrible. It was all over Snapchat and it even got to the point where someone's life was threatened.

That is where I met her. She and her community at the school had banned together to get the student code of conduct changed. She later went on to write poetry as a form of protest and to get involved in activism she published her own book. She did all that because of her involvement with Fenix. I watched her go through hell, and that night at the bar where I ran into her, she was updating me on her life, and she told me she was now working with kids thanks to me. Personally, I was not big in being called a mentor because there is a stigma that comes with it. I prefer a trusted adult. But knowing that I have left a heavy impact on her and so many others that have gone and branched out to do so many remarkable things makes me feel amazing.

Seeing these adults that I have known since they were kids, that didn't come from the prettiest neighborhoods or have the access to all the resources to do what they were put here to do, which is to make a difference, makes my heart so warm and full. Knowing that since I pursued my passion, others can and will too makes it all worth it in the end.

A New Chapter

Janet Eke's Story as Told to Mekhi Armstrong

Three hours away!? That was how far it took to drive down the Eastern Shore of Maryland. I didn't even think there was an Eastern Shore to Maryland. Well, that's not true, of course. There's East, North, South, and West everywhere. What I mean to say is that I hadn't *thought* about Maryland's Eastern Shore. I was always a city girl. From Boston, Massachusetts to Fairfax, Virginia, I always occupied an urban space. But Princess Anne was so different. As I drove down that massive Bay Bridge that seemed entirely too long, and entered endless roads passing fields of golden grain, I was astounded by how different it was to the city.

If it weren't for this job, I wouldn't even have discovered this side of Maryland. But that's what life is all about, new discoveries. As a librarian, the thirst for learning always enticed me. The thrill of turning the next page in a book to see what happens next. I first started working as a librarian at The University of Maryland Eastern Shore right around the beginning of Covid-19. When I settled on Princess Anne, I turned the page, and started this new chapter in my life.

I moved to Princess Anne around 2019. It was just me and my two sons, one of whom had already graduated college before we moved; the other was a freshman at Johns Hopkins. Due to quarantine, it was

11

tough to find a community for myself. Unlike the inhospitable people of Boston, Princess Anne natives were much kinder. I would spend hours talking with my neighbors from our porches and learn a lot about the people I lived around. I did not know of things to do out in Salisbury. For starters, everything was a drive compared to the city where things were a lot more accessible. I began attending different activities in town to better acquaint myself with the area: going to church, learning about the town's history from historical events, and even talking more with the people I worked with, all of which helped me settle in faster than I would have expected. The history of the town is especially fascinating because I noticed how much it tied together with UMES history. There is a lot of racial history in Princess Anne that was new to me. It was once a town that was heavily against black people and they held a lot of animosity toward the idea of a school for black college students being built in town. Even now because of that history, I noticed that the town and campus community between UMES was very lacking. I even learned in the attic of the church I attended that there was a place where black slaves sat. Perhaps this is why the town and school community are so divided.

During Covid is when I noticed the library really starting to become a center of community on campus. Because of social distancing, people weren't congregating as much, but they would still go to the library. It gave students a place that was open, allowing students to keep their distance and also get outside of the confines of their dorm rooms. These days, it's not as busy. Did you know that at one point the library was once the center of campus? This began to change as more newer buildings were constructed on campus, like the engineering building and the pharmacy building. They have a lot of access to technological labs and whatnot that allow students to access knowledge in one space. Many would say, due to these new technological expansions within these new facilities, the library may not hold as much importance. To that I say, that is simply not true.

Many people aren't aware that these digital resources are purchased and maintained by the library. It reflects today's reality that the library is both a physical and a virtual space. As far as the growth of technology, I am all for it. The library must embrace and leverage new technology. In fact, the library is actively transitioning from a print world to a digital world. We have twice as many ebooks as print books and thousands more eJournals than print journals. I mean we already dedicate our lives to gathering knowledge in whatever its form, so it makes sense that we should already be involved. Even when

Google first started, I felt that librarians should have been essential to this process. It is we who are experts at organizing and curating information. I think it would also get students more engaged in coming to the library more, although the decline in foot traffic into the library does not really concern me since usage of digital resources remains robust and continues to increase. I think by playing a bigger role on campus, we help unite both students and faculty alike to be more involved in the passing of knowledge.

I found my community in Princess Anne working as a librarian at UMES' Frederick Douglass Library. As someone who has lived in multiple cities, I am very fortunate that I was able to find belonging in such a different environment. Being part of a foundation that helps the new generation grow is a beautiful thing that I couldn't be more proud of. I encourage everyone to visit the local library every once in a while. Who knows what you might find?

THE PULL OF THE SHORE

JOCELYN BRIDDELL'S STORY AS TOLD TO DANNY JO PUWO

G rowing up in the vibrant state of New Jersey, my childhood was colored with memories of Berlin, where my dad's family lived from Worcester County. The holidays were always a special time, as I eagerly anticipated the joy of Christmas and the warmth of Thanksgiving, surrounded by my beloved grandparents. Little did I know then that those cherished moments would guide my life's journey, leading me back to the shores I hold so dear.

I am the first born of two children to my parents; my mom was an opera singer and my dad was a United Methodist minister, so my early ages were one of a kind I would say. Growing up I would listen to my mom rehearse every chance I could. Our love for opera was so great. Every Saturday at 1:00pm we listened to The Metropolitan Opera House on the radio which expanded my knowledge about the art. Although I didn't always understand the language, I would sit with the libretto for a particular opera and follow along making me familiar with what was going on without knowing the language. I learned to love it. My dad, as a United Methodist Minister, would travel a lot all around the world to spread the Word through books and films for children about the Christian faith. My dad knew Desmond Tutu and Martin Luther King Jr. as he went to school with Dr. King. We traveled throughout the United States and even Europe. In fact, I studied in

15

Geneva for 8 months when I was 13. There, I had to learn French to be able to move about. Another memorable trip was in Italy, where I got the opportunity to meet Desmond Tutu, which also was the first time we saw a video camera. This was back in 1972 and it's funny because look at how much we can do with technology now.

I grew up in New Jersey for the most part of my life. I loved my community so much. Teaneck began integrating its schools before receiving a court order making it a place where great relationships were built. I think it was a really good way to demonstrate that we are one as people and there was no need for the separation in the first place. After high school, I went on to college in New Jersey to major in American studies and African studies which was something I had a passion for at the time. In college, I was really involved in political issues. I grew up at a time when there were civil rights demonstrations and women's rights as well as protests against the Vietnam War and apartheid in South Africa. Apartheid was still being practiced in South Africa so we protested my university so it would divest its funds through campaigns and marches.

My career started in 1983 after I graduated from grad school and worked at colleges in student affairs. I stepped out of the education sector in 2013 and I worked at a nonprofit in Nashville for seven years and in 2020 Dr. Lane, director of the UMES Honors Program, hired me to be the Assistant Director.

I first came back to the shore in 2019 to spend time with my father who was suffering from dementia. He later passed in 2022, and I had now lost two people I loved dearly: my younger brother when I was 29 and now my dad. Losing my dad made me value family more than I already did. I thought to myself, I have already accomplished a lot, inherited a house in Berlin 15 years ago, and I wanted to be closer to family. And I didn't like Nashville politics very much, which was where I lived, so coming to the shore to help care for my dad came at a perfect time.

I will always treasure the time I spent at UMES working with honors students. Working with the honors students and helping them with their academics was the fun part of the job. It wasn't without difficulties, though. I always felt the honors program wasn't doing enough and during my time I tried to implement as much as possible, but there was only so much I could do with my position. I felt we should have had more workshops, travels, and many more activities and opportunities for the students. I mean they worked hard to get here and what were the benefits of their hard work? I just felt I was the only one amongst colleagues who really cared enough to put in the work. The absence of a common resolve led to an underlying sense of discord that occasionally masked the joyful experiences.

What I always wanted my students to understand was to learn all you can in your undergrad experience, travel, go abroad— there is so much you can learn from being in someone else's country. College sets your foundation for the rest of your life. Enjoy your time and take advantage as much as you can.

Raised by UMES

Etahe Johnson's Story as Told to Deanna Morgan

U MES raised me. I remember being a little kid and going to work with my mom and dad. They both worked at the University of Maryland Eastern Shore—my dad, a professor in the English department, and my mom working in the admissions office. I remember being little and my mom waking me up at 8 o'clock in the morning and packing my stuff up to go to work with her. I used to sit in the office and help her answer the phones and sometimes file paperwork, too. My mom and dad weren't the only ones who worked at the school. My brother was the campus barber and my niece also worked there. I just didn't think that I would be a part of the family legacy, too.

I originally lived in Salisbury, growing up my whole life surrounded by my family, but when I graduated high school and it was time for me to go to college, I decided to go to North California University. My dad had graduated from there when he was going to school and I always wanted to go ever since. This was a chance to be on my own, away from my parents to gain freedom and grow. My freshman year taught me a lot of things about myself. I got good grades, but I was also out partying and having a good time. By the end of that year, I realized I needed to work on my discipline.

After graduating and continuing my education by getting my undergrad, I ended up moving to Iowa for my graduate level. When I was out there, I landed a job that was comfortable for some time. I ended up spending 15 years out there before deciding to move back to Salisbury. I was trying to fight off going into teaching for the longest time before moving back. I had a conversation with my dad and he said "Aren't you tired of getting laid off by corporate America? I know one area that you can go into that we will always need and that's teaching." As much as I didn't want to go into teaching, after a couple of hours going back and forth, I caved in, and ended up teaching at UMES. At first, I wasn't sure about it, but ended up falling in love with it. Seeing the students every day and learning everyone's name, who they were, and their hopes and dreams. After starting my new job on campus, I also fell in love and met the love of my life, my fiancé, who was also my mom's work-study student when he went to school here.

I have seen how some things have changed. I had a student that had gotten evicted. I didn't know that he had gotten evicted because he was coming to class every day. It wasn't until one day I saw him walking and somebody said "Hey, you know that your student doesn't have a room or anything?" Finding this out made me very upset, and I started to think of what I could do to help. I began to make some phone calls and was actually able to get him housing and a meal plan after talking to the Director of Housing. This story stuck with me for years after. This wasn't the only time a case like this transpired, this is just the one that stuck out to me the most.

Being here at UMES for so long I have observed a lot over the years. I can honestly say that the students and community have gotten away from each other. I say this because there used to be a strong presence with the students in the community, and overall helping the students reach their full potential in a safe learning environment. I remember we used to help students with clothes, food, housing, financial aid, and anything that they needed, but now that the years have gone by it's like we're in a different society. I remember being younger, walking all around UMES campus every day. I used to walk to the storefronts and the downtown area. Nowadays all of that has changed. The stores don't look the same anymore. Apart from that, the weather, the climate here has changed, which makes it difficult for some of the students to get to where they need to go. Overall, I hope to reunite the bridge between the students and the community. I hope to make UMES great again!

LOVE'S IMPACT

NIKKI BLAKE'S STORY AS TOLD TO DENAYA FREEMAN

I 've overcome a lot as a teen mother in the 12th grade. Though it wasn't chosen, my career was what best suited me. Have you ever seized an opportunity without hesitation? Some people were doubters, while others had faith in me. People tend to evaluate a person by their cover, which is especially true for me as a proud Black woman principal. But even among the bad folks, there was always a bright side. I constantly try to have a big influence on other people. I had people that believed in me, so why not influence others as well? I came to have a unique perspective after I became a principal. Dr. Kim Purris was my #1 supporter during it all. After graduating from Salisbury University with a bachelor's degree in elementary education, I went on to the University of Phoenix to earn a master's degree in administrative supervision. I then returned and completed my doctorate in educational leadership.

As I grew older, I engaged in a bunch of different aspects of the school system from being a teacher, to working in administration, and eventually becoming the principal of Wicomico High School. I've helped all different grade levels. To me, high school caught my biggest interest. The motto that I go by here at Wi-High with all my students and staff workers is: core, support and structure. Core implies focusing on the bottom line within everyone. Support indicates helping and advocating for all. Structure is very self-explanatory; it's what's best in today's time. This is a need vs. a want. Here at Wi-High, everyone needs their own love. When I say everyone, I speak upon my tribe. My tribe is my students and staff. Everyone gets a different type of love depending on what they need. Some students are motherless and need a mommy figure. This role made me establish myself more as a leader because I became more fluent in what they needed and helped with different tasks at various times. Working with children has made me find community. I fit right in from student improvement, working within my one tribe, living in my past and feeling like a kid again, but mostly loving my job and what I do for the staff and students. I never take off work unless I necessarily must.

I find community within myself and with my students by showing leadership, loving my job, and having nostalgic moments on specific things I have done compared to what they're doing at this age. Another aspect of me finding community with my students is watching my students improve. Dealing with children for so long has given me a changed mindset and to move differently about things because being a leader, my tribe will follow me. With this being my second year here as principal at Wi-High, I am very appreciative of the students being very vulnerable to me and trusting me with everything they have told me. Scouts honor!

My career was chosen for me to work with teenage adolescents and young adults. Middle and high schoolers know right from wrong. Collaborating with toddlers and elementary schoolers is too much like babysitting and making sure they are learning the bare minimum. If I had to switch my loving place of work, I wouldn't. I absolutely love it here. I love it here so much; I give out the love that the students need. This place vs. any other school in the country, I will always choose Wi-High.

I am in a terrific place right now because I love what I do for a living, I keep up with my tribe, and I continue to grow as a leader to better serve my students. I still intend to continue having an influence on my tribe in the years to come. No one should ever be nasty, no matter where they come from, but people are ruder and braver these days. I would love to change that narrative with my leadership abilities. Success both here and at home causes additional friction, but I'm going to keep improving and acting in my own, and my people's, best interests.

MY MOTIVE

KADEEM TURNBULL'S STORY AS TOLD TO ALEXA BEAUFORD

A t my master's graduation, I still didn't feel accomplished. I wanted more. The other colors of the graduation gowns caught my eye. I looked at the gown and I said "I want that gown." I wondered what degree it was for. They said it was for educational leadership, so I asked my friend if I could join the organization's leadership program. She recommended that I talk to the professor. After talking with the professor, I found out that I could put the application in, but I wouldn't be able to join until the next school year. I wasn't planning on sitting around and not doing anything for a full year. I believe that's how you fall out of school and don't want to fall back into it. I said no. I knew I was not doing that.

I learned very early on to stop planning. My goal was to go to law school after I graduated with my bachelor's degree. My professor recommended the master's program in criminal justice since I was graduating early. He said "why don't you see where it takes you?" I applied to the doctorate program. While in the interview, the professor said, "Kadeem, let me share something with you. I typically don't accept students like you into my program." I'm like where is he going with this? I have a good enough grade point average, so what's the matter?

The professor agreed and said it's something that you wrote that made me want to give you this opportunity. I wrote that I wanted to be the youngest Jamaican prime minister. I felt that he saw the ambition there. He went into details and said "I want to tell you something to never forget, that is humility. Someone helped you get to where you are, therefore you must help the next person get to where they need to be."

As I entered the University of Maryland Eastern Shore, my area director was my mentor. He had a major influence on my career. When my dad had dropped me off, he said to stick with this man. He believed that he would take me places, and he did. He provided guidance which kept me on a narrow path. He has a good heart and he gives so much more than he receives. The campus needs more of him. I always give thanks to him for all that he has done for me. So, in 2013, I came to the university and finished my undergraduate in three years. I have been a resident assistant, student director, and served in a student residential complex. In 2016, I started my master's program and moved to Salisbury. I was commuting every day to school and on Sunday to church. I spent one year working at the airport while being a part-time senior RA on campus. Then I returned to the campus full-time as a graduate assistant for a year. From there, I went to area director for two years. Around 2019, I applied for a new position. I moved to Crisfield for two years and in March of 2020, I got my first call. In July 2020, in the midst of Covid, I got hired. I am currently the Director of Alumni Relations and Special Events.

In all my positions I have worked, I have always tried to find a way to help and offer something that nobody else is offering. I feel that being an alumnus of the university helped a lot because I understand the culture, geography, and how diverse the school is. I try to remember that not everybody is going to feel the same way about the school as I do. It's my job to be the best I can in serving. I know when to step away from the desk and do my diligence if a student needs direction or advice. For example, I knew a student who would make a good actor. Therefore, I taught a theater class for three semesters while he was here. I saw that he had a gift and I showed him a different pathway. The student is continuously growing in different ways due to him being open-minded. The University has developed me, too. When I came to the campus, I made myself a promise knowing that the school was taking a chance on me. I said to myself in the same breath, I am going to give the University all that I have until God tells me it's time to go.

26

Funny story, I wasn't even going to attend UMES, but when my counselor brought up historically Black universities, University of Maryland Eastern Shore seemed like a good fit for me. I applied thinking the campus was beautiful and huge. I did all my research and was calling the school. It was like I was attending before I even got there. I had an academic scholarship that would cover the cost of schooling. Although, my advice would be to not worry about the cost. Many times, students burden themselves with the bill. An educational bill is going to put you in a percentile that's going to have you doing way better than your peers in the next ten years. Somebody who has just a high school diploma could have the same work ethic, intelligence quotient, and potential as you do, but the one thing they don't have is that degree. That degree puts you on a higher pedestal. You don't always see the outcome of when you invest in yourself right away, but the foundation is built though.

Bridge to a Better Future

Carrie Samis's Story as Told to McKenzie Abiley

I grew up in the Delmarva area, and I moved specifically to Princess Anne maybe six or seven years ago. I actually live right downtown in the Main Street District where I work. Before I moved there, I was living at Pemberton Park in a historic house on the river in Salisbury. It's a 270-acre county park and the county decided to no longer have tenants on their three-park property. At the time I was working in Worcester County, and I was going to Princess Anne a lot and I had actually always loved Somerset County. I like the naturalistic elements and that I can be near the river and nature trails and in 30 minutes be at the beach and in the ocean. Some local Historical Society people reached out to me to ask if I could help them find a tenant for one of their historic homes here. I was living in a historic home in Salisbury, and then as it happened, that property was no longer available. So, it was a great opportunity for me because I needed somewhere to live, and I am already fond of and accustomed to Somerset County.

When I first moved here and started working as Main Street Director, a lot of the buildings here in Princess Anne were vacant. Since I started in my position, in the last four years or so, we've had at least 17 new businesses open. We have a beautiful historic downtown district and the work that I do provides help to promote businesses, programs at the university, and programs the town and other agencies are doing in order to help to foster that sense of community. I actually had no idea I would end up in this profession. I was a philosophy major at SU, and I also had a strong background in biology and English, and oddly religion— comparative religion, and so everything I did really focused on nature, culture, and community. I didn't really know what I wanted to do at the time, but while I was in college and shortly after, I volunteered for causes, agencies, and organizations that I was passionate about. That evolved into a career that has focused on environmental conservation and natural and cultural heritage. I've worked only in nonprofit organizations and for small local government agencies, but always focused on either the environment, people, or some combination of the two. Working now for our Main Street District here in Princess Anne, I find it's unique from all other districts in our state because of the diversity we embody. Almost all of our businesses are owned and operated by women, people of color, and immigrants, which wasn't always the case.

This was a very segregated district and a lot of the buildings that we're in today were not accessible to people of color. Elected officials of the town government were almost exclusively white and mostly men. Previously, there had been a kind of division between the town and government relations; students were discouraged from crossing the railroad track for coming to town. There's still this kind of racial tension in the community in some ways, but things have shifted drastically. Even the makeup of our elected officials has changed. Now, we have a majority Black Council and a majority Black staff which is what you should see in a community that's 75% African American. There are still meetings that I go to where I'm the only woman there, but change is still happening. Now that more women and people of color are in positions where they can make changes, change is happening for the better.

I'm very active in seeking grant funding to help support the businesses downtown and to help provide resources to the community. I am aiming to work closely with the university to develop new ideas and pursue new avenues for funding that would benefit the university students, staff, the town, and town residents as well. We all work much more closely together now to promote events that we're a part of. We were just off the Seagull Century, which is over 3000...3500 bicyclists ride right through town. It's super hokey, but we have volunteers that make signs and stand on the side of the street to cheer them on, we hire a DJ, and we have bubbles and it's just silly but cool. The great part about hosting these events is that it brings people back to our community. A lot of the Century riders come back to visit our town to eat and shop here. We also get a lot of volunteers from staff and students at UMES, and that expands the human footprint in the community so that people in the community see them and see UMES as connected and whatever we can do to solidify that connection, we do.

One of the things that I really want is to create a better walkway, like a physical connector between the university and downtown. People can ride their bikes, skateboard, walk, whatever. Something that brings people from campus to downtown and brings people who live in our community to campus, because I think there's still people in the community that don't necessarily spend time on campus. Our community has come a long way in a sense of embodying diversity and making connections to other communities outside of our own, but my goal is to really create that true connection between our community and the university.

HOW THE TABLES HAVE TURNED

MICHAEL BROWNE'S STORY AS TOLD TO CHARLES SMITH III

B orn and raised in North Philadelphia, life had plenty of opportunities, but somehow, things were still hard early on. I entered grade school, where the majority of my peers were Black. Surrounded by those that looked like me, initially gave me a feeling of comfort and connection. Time went on, and I soon realized that that wasn't the case. Going about my elementary years of grade school, there were some teachers and educators that treated me as if I wasn't wanted in their classroom or even at the school in general. As a young Black child, with what *some* would call a "normal" lifestyle for Black people, I was seen as less. Just less. Everywhere I went, I walked around believing I was less. Being so young, so vulnerable, so innocent, why am I any less than the person beside me? They say consistency is key. But to what? As far as I'm concerned, I have plenty of constant negative talk, constant negative energy, constant neglect, all of which is targeted at me. But this key isn't brightening my future any. Or is it?

I continued going through school, year after year, dealing with this mental abuse from the ones who are supposed to do quite the opposite for young kids. Middle school came, and something changed. There was a slight shift that came across in my academics. I was no longer looked at as that Black kid who came from a typical Black family, that boy who "probably won't...," that student who was different and

33

unwelcomed. I was now that young man who has a bright future, that young man who "most likely will...," that young man who had so much to offer no matter the color of his skin. I had people, teachers, who actually believed in me. And from this point on, I knew what I wanted to do once I grew up.

My middle school era helped me uncover all of that mental decay that was laid on me. I began to find out things about myself like being musically inclined. I found out what kind of influence I wanted to make as I grew older. And most importantly, I found out that I was exactly like everyone else: a human with God-given gifts, hard times along the road, and a future to create. I was bound for change. I was able to go to high school for the arts, and there were two things I didn't play about. One, my growth as a person and in my education, and two, band. I would never miss a band day. Even on sick days, I was never sick enough to not attend band. It wasn't just a passion of mine; band and percussion was my therapy, a time where I could drop everything and clear my mind. On days I didn't have band, I found myself often helping others and giving back. This helped me learn how to read, understand, and apply to those in need. Knowing I wanted to become an educator back in late elementary/early middle school, educating and mentoring came naturally on a daily basis. It became something I enjoyed doing so often. With my eyes set and brain knowing what this world needs, I set off to do just that.

A few years down the line, I found myself working down on the shore. This was after I had declined their first offer from over a year ago. Somehow, I managed to stay on their minds to where they reached back out with the same interest. They say culture shock, and indeed it was. The shore was very different from the city in Pennsylvania. Felt like nowhere, but somewhere at the same time. First impressions were that this is a good place to raise a family. Not much commotion, noise, and daily dangers like the city. I'm kinda catching a liking for this little spot. I quickly realized how different growing up was here than back where I'm from. The opportunities are slim to none, and many find the streets as their place after high school. What can I do to help change this?

Even with all of the opportunities my hometown had, I still had a rough beginning. Crazy thing is, a lot of these kids have the same beginnings, just with less opportunities. From there, I knew how I could connect with these children. What I needed is what I was to them. Growing from position to position, and seeing more and more kids from all areas of life, I wanted and needed a place where I could reach everyone and not just a set few. However, with my set few, I began to connect with parents, and community members through the world of my students. At this time, a wise lady told me that the best way to become a part of a community is to live in the community. And that's exactly what I did.

As soon as I moved, the comfort from students and parents swept in immediately. Kids would come to my house just to chat, parents would give me a call, and the community knew who I was. Always consistent. Always consistent. That's what I live by. That's how I run things. Never let someone run across me and not gain something. I was made to be that light in the darkness of those young children. The one that allows them to be themselves with no regret. The bridge that connects their possible future to their present.

A COMMUNITY BUILT FROM WITHIN

TIARA CORNELIUS'S STORY AS TOLD TO SOPHIA I. CRUZADO

I t is often the smallest of actions that lead to the largest of changes. I began my life on the Eastern Shore of Virginia, a place that was unbelievably more rural than the next town I lived in. I moved at the age of ten to Princess Anne, Maryland, a town that holds historical and cultural heritage. I remember it being the second home where my family and I would be living...but the first home that had been built specifically for us. This home was within a small town that is known for their community-oriented atmosphere. I stayed in the area from the age of ten up until the age of twenty. My connection to the city stemmed from my upbringing, and my desire to remain close to home stemmed from my parents. I allowed myself the opportunity to create some distance between the shore and me—but only enough for me to explore life. It was very important to me that my parents were close enough for me to see, but far enough for me to branch out.

My parents were my support system—my home. Whenever I was experiencing a crisis, they made themselves available. My parents always knew how to help soothe me, and because of that, I always knew I needed to keep them close by—just in case anything happened. It took me a while to understand why these feelings were always so strong, and that they were ultimately being caused by anxiety. Anxiety is something that, at a young age, I never realized I had or could ever experience. It wasn't until the spring of 2020, when the COVID-19 pandemic erupted, that I realized it was time to take care of my mental health. Similar to others, going into lockdown was a very traumatic experience for me. Before the pandemic, I considered myself an introvert, but after being forced to be an introvert at all times for a long period of time, I realized that I was only an introvert by choice. This meant that I enjoyed and mentally benefited from being able to choose when I did or did not isolate myself from social factors. Forced isolation made me realize that I needed to be close to and around my friends, loved ones, and my students.

My students are the reason why I do not feel the need to have children of my own. My students *are* my children. During the pandemic, I worried about a lot of my students and what their lives at home would be like. I was aware that some of them did not come from the safest backgrounds, and that a lot of them had found themselves while being away from home and at college. Some of my students, having to hide their identities while being forced home for an unknown long period of time, also contributed to my anxiety. I thought about my students who did not have consistent access to food and how being away from campus, without a plan that allowed them to have consistent meals, would affect their health. I can admit that I was more worried about my students than myself–worried that they would be feeling the same suffocation that I was experiencing at the time.

My students are my favorite thing about living on the shore. Even when they get on my nerves, as a child sometimes would to their parents, I find myself caring and wanting to protect them. Sometimes it becomes frustrating when I see them make some bad decisions that I already made when I was their age. I want to be able to run to them and express that I have already been down that road and that I would hate to see them experience the same outcomes that I did. But I cannot. I cannot tell them not to do something because, sometimes, when you tell someone to go left, they still choose to go right because you instructed them to do otherwise. It is a canon event that I cannot interrupt. Some experiences, no matter how small, shape who we will become in the future.

The closeness that UMES allows faculty to have with each other and our students allows us to build higher connections and closer bonds that larger universities sometimes cannot access. When I have met with faculty members of other institutions, I would recognize a pattern within the complaints. Some instructors were saying that they felt bad for not being able to connect with their students. The lack of connection created a gap between the instructor and the student, which limited the access a student needed to get help to succeed. When I began my career, a major goal of mine was to make sure that students developed the required math skills needed. I knew that I would do anything that was needed to help a student increase their chances of success, both in and out of my classroom. I can say that I have worked hard to reach that goal and that the majority of my students had successful outcomes.

It is important for my colleagues and I to build the next workforce that will, in the future, take our places and teach the upcoming generations. To contribute to this goal, I will soon be stepping into the role of Executive Director of STEM Stars. STEM Stars is a program whose focus is to increase the number of students of color, particularly African-American students, who will receive PhDs in STEM areas. It is extremely important for the generation after me to continue to be able to pursue higher education and receive PhDs. By taking action and stepping into this role, my colleagues and I can work as both a society and an HBCU to give the proper access, support, and guidance to students. It is our responsibility to allow students to feel like they can come home, to a place that will soothe them and where a support system will always be available.

STORYTELLERS & WRITERS

Mckenzie Abiley

Mekhi Armstrong

Alexa Beauford

Nikki Blake

Jocelyn Briddell

Michael Browne

Adin Clarke

Tiara Cornelius

Sophia I. Cruzado

Janet Eke

Denaya Freeman

Cameron Geddie

Amber Green

Earl Holland

Dayauni Jeffries

Etahe Johnson

James Jones

Angel Mansfield

Deanna Morgan

Danny Jo Puwo

Carrie Samis

Charles Smith III

Kadeem Turnbull

QUESTIONS FOR DISCUSSION

1. How did education, specifically the community fostered by your educational environment, help foster a bridge to a better future for you?

2. What is the "single story" told about your community, and how have the individual narratives you have heard from other community members helped to fracture that to form a more complete or prismatic view?

3. What role do you see technology playing as a means of creating and futurizing community, especially in rural locations?

4. What are some of the overlapping intersections of community partnerships you have and how do they complement each other in terms of building your growth?

5. How do you find the geography of certain places pulls us toward a single story, and how do we best combat that to achieve a fuller, richer narrative of place-based identity?

6. Many of these stories feature an obstacle that was overcome and how community became a propellant to help achieve one's goal. How have you individually overcome an obstacle with the help of the collective?

7. What are some of the common barriers to establishing

community that exist at both the town/community level and the gown/collegiate level? How can we work to overcome them and is there an opportunity for crossover here? How?

8. Where are the communities of hope? What does the future of community building look like moving forward?

9. Relate a moment where hearing someone else's story helped grow your own perspective and your own empathy. Share your story here: https://facingproject.com/how-to-share-my-story/

10. How has the changing collegiate experience (from when your parents were in school to when you attended) helped or hindered community-building? How do you see towns with a college at their center including the collegiate community and vice-versa?

DISCUSSING THIS TOPIC IN YOUR COMMUNITY

Because The Facing Project is steeped in empathy and connecting across differences, *Listening Circles* are a fantastic way to bring more people into the conversation on the topics/themes addressed in this book.

Listening Circles provide readers with a more intimate experience to reflect upon the stories and ask questions in a controlled environment. However, it's important to include a trained facilitator who understands how to moderate, when to let conversations flow, and when to step in to move them along.

If you choose to include *Listening Circles* in your community, we recommend having at least four different locations and dates for these to happen, and be sure to have folks register in advance. Hosts could include area libraries, schools, and/or colleges and universities.

Also, it's important to set the following standards at the beginning of each discussion:

1. We acknowledge that we are all here to learn with open hearts and open minds.

2. Before speaking or asking a question, we all agree that we will take a moment to reflect on if "my voice/question matters in

the particular moment" or if "I should give the opportunity to someone else to speak."

3. R-E-S-P-E-C-T is more than an Aretha Franklin song; respect is a value that we will hold close throughout our discussions.

4. We honor the storytellers who shared their experiences, and our goal is to not discount them but rather to understand how all of our stories are intertwined and part of the human condition.

Ideally, *Listening Circles* should have no more than 20 participants in each circle. If you find that one of your locations may have more than 20, you'll want to explore breaking them up into more than one group.

Also, participants should have read a copy of this book before participating. This makes for deeper discussion, and it keeps the facilitators from having to give a full breakdown of all of the themes/topics included throughout the book. More copies can be ordered at www.facingproject.com.

However, it's always good to open a *Listening Circle* with a reading of one or two stories that immediately follow introductions and community standards. Ask for one to two attendees to volunteer to read the selected stories aloud to the *Circle*.

Then have the facilitator ask the group: How did those two stories make you feel?

And be sure to have them follow-up with "tell me more" and other open-ended questions. Of course, a trained facilitator will understand how to let this process flow.

Lastly, be sure to include action items for the participants. This could include other events in your community centered around the topic/issues addressed in this book, volunteer opportunities with nonprofits, and/or other ways they can get involved.

SPONSORS

About The Facing Project

The Facing Project is a 501(c)(3) nonprofit that creates a more understanding and empathetic world through stories that inspire action. The organization provides tools and a platform for everyday individuals to share their stories, connect across differences, and begin conversations using their own narratives as a guide. The Facing Project has engaged more than 7,500 volunteer storytellers, writers, and actors who have told more than 1,500 stories that have been used in grassroots movements, in schools, and in government to inform and inspire action. In addition, stories from The Facing Project are published in books through The Facing Project Press and are regularly performed on *The Facing Project Radio Show* on NPR.

- Learn more at facingproject.com.

- Follow us on Twitter and Instagram @FacingProject, and on Facebook at *TheFacingProject*.

Milton Keynes UK
Ingram Content Group UK Ltd.
UKHW010841190424
441445UK00001B/53

9 798986 096193